Little Guy

by

RJ Huston

Good morning, Little Guy.
It's time to wake up.

Little Guy, you're such a cute pup.

Little Guy, it's funny when you lick my nose.

Ouch! Little Guy, why do you bite my toes?

Oh, Little Guy, don't eat rocks.

No!
Little Guy,
let go
of my
sock!

Little Guy, why do you like things that are smelly?
SIKE

No, Little Guy, get off the table and out of the jelly!

Little Guy, stop trying to eat bugs.

Little Guy, no! We don't do that on rugs.

Little Guy, stop playing
with ants.

Little Guy, don't dig up the plants!

Little Guy, don't make so much noise!

Little Guy,
please be
quiet
and play
with your
toys.

Little Guy, you finally got tired
and stretched out on the floor.

For a little
guy, you sure
do have a
loud snore.

Little Guy,
goodnight and
let your dreams
begin.

Little Guy, tomorrow, you get to do it all over again.